SKIN HEALTH PRODUCT STRATEGY

JOHN LOK

ISBN 979-888591446-8

Contents

Preface

Introduction

Nowadays, there are many face skin health product sale in face skin health market. So, there are many different kinds of facial health product choices to let health product users to choose, it brings the skin health product competition is serious. How to avoid the raising competition threats and facial health product buyers spend more time to choose many different skin health products in their choice process. Hence, how to achieve effective market promotion strategy is very important to any kinds of face skin health protection products.

In my this book , I shall indicate different kinds of promotion methods to let different kinds of face skin health protection products to choose which of promotion strategy is the most suitable to help them to promote their unique skin health protection products to sell more easily in nowadays skin health product market. Readers can have more clear understanding how and why the kind of promotion method is the most suitable to let the kind of skin health product to advertise to let face skin health consumers have more clear understanding to its face skin health protection function.

Prologue

CHAPTER ONE

Body shop facial health promotion method

The body shop international power line carrier (the body shop) was founded by Dame Anita Roddick in the England in 1976. It sold personal beauty care products, such as baby and child specific products, bath and shower and colour cosmetics, deodorants, skin care, hair care, fragrances, sun care etc skin health products to provide human body benefits. Nowadays, the body shop was skin and body care manufacturer and retailer operating in 55 countries with over 2,100 stores. It had 42 exclusive outlets in Hong Kong. It's missions were to dedicate to pursuit of social and environment change to meaningfully contribute to local, national and international communities in which trade to passionately campaign for the protection of the environment, human and civil rights and against animal testing and to make fun, passion and care part of our daily lives (Adrian, P. 2012).

● What is the difference between production orientation and societal marketing orientation and sales orientation

There are five main marketing orientations of which a company will adopt one. This will determine the way it interacts with the customer. Such as product orientation suggests that a company focuses inwards looking at what it is capable of, rather than the needs and wants of the client; sales orientation is based upon selling existing products with a turnover sale numbers relationship marketing orientation recognizes the value of repeat business over, not only with customers but suppliers as well; societal marketing orientation is relatively new in the scheme of things but suggests on top of meeting the needs and wants of the customer and the organization there is the societies interests to be looked and marketing orientation is based around the needs and wants of a customer to meet business objectives and it assumes that a sale depends on a customer's decision to purchase a product or provide a service.

Marketing can be seen at two levels, the first level is such as a business philosophy, marketing puts customers at the center of an organization's consideration and which is reflected in basic values , such as the requirement to understand and respond to customers' needs and the necessary to search constantly for new market opportunity. In a truly marketing oriented organization, these values are instilled in all employees and should influence their behavior without any need for prompting. The personnel manager would have a selection policy that recruited staff who could fulfil the needs of customers rather than simply minimizing the wage bill in any marketing oriented organization. The other level is techniques of marketing also include pricing, the design of channels of distribution and new product development.

The assessing the nature and importance of market orientation for large firms, such as body shop. The three components of market orientation could be analytically separated. The components of market orientation organization include the first component is the customer orientation, it means an organization must have a thorough understanding of its target buyers, so that it can create a product of superior value to give client benefits ; the second component is the competitor orientation, it means any firm should look at how well its competitors are able to satisfy buyers' needs. It should understand the short term strengths and weaknesses and long term capabilities and strategies of current and potential competitors as well as the third component is to develop marketing plans that are not acted upon by people who are capable of delivering promises made to customers and a marketing orientation organization requires that the organization draws upon and integrates its human and physical resources effectively and adapts them to meet client's needs. Otherwise, a production and sales orientation may be appropriate to firms at certain stages in the evolution of markets. Where the dominant business environment is based on the need for good production planning above all, the company that does this best will achieve the greatest overall business success. It is either production orientation, it means organizations that produce what they imagined consumers wanted, rather than what they actually wanted. Planning for full utilization of capital equipment are often seen as more important than ensuring that equipment is used to provide goods and services that people actually wants. Production-oriented firms generally aim for efficiency in production rather than effectiveness in meeting customer's needs . It is either or selling orientation, it means advertising, sales promotion and personal selling techniques are used to emphasize product differentiation and brands and it does not focus on satisfying client needs or desire new product offerings and production led. Hence, one market orientation organization needs to focus on satisfying clients' needs profitably by these marketing mix, such as product, price, place, physical evidence, processed, people and promotion. Anyway ,Market orientation implied that body shop , which ought seek information about clients, such as current and future needs and took action based this information (client orientation); it ought seek information about competitors' current strengths and weaknesses and their long term strategies and took actions based on these information (competitor orientation) ; it ought coordinate the actions taken by sharing clients and competitors information internally (intra-firm communication).

The three components of market orientation meant social marketing and understanding boarder concerns and ethical environmental, legal and social context of marketing activities and programs. The cause and effects of marketing clearly beyond the company and the consumer to society as whole. New terms humanistic marketing and ecological marketing were suggested to societal marketing concept.The social marketing concept holds that the organization's task is to determine the needs, wants and interests of target markets and to deliver the desired satisfactions more effectively and efficiently than competitors and the society's welling being, such as body shop had achieved sales and profit gains by adopting and practicing a form of the societal marketing concept called cause related marketing.

● DISCUSSION OF BODY SHOP HEALTH PRODUCT PROMOTION STRATEGY

Body Shop is marketing orientation organization in 30 years. Critically assess the extent to which I consider Body Shop to be a truly marketing oriented organization throughout its 30 years history . It seemed body shop had achieved cause-related marketing as an opportunity to enhance their corporate reputation, raised brand awareness, increased customer loyalty and built sales.

It's corporate values were composed of five core values. The first one was to oppose animal testing. The opposing animal testing for both cosmetic products and ingredients began in 1976 years.

In the 1980 year and 1990 year, who successfully campaigned with animal protection groups to change the UK and European laws to support the development products were tried on human

volunteers. Along with the development of technology testing had played a leading role to protect the rights of both human and animals . The second one was to support community trade, it initiated the trade not aid objective of creating trade to help people in the third world utilizing their resources to their own needs. This reflects communities needed a fair price for natural ingredients who purchased from these often marginalized countries. The third one was to activate self esteem. Women were the main customers and employees in the body shop. The fourth one was to defend human rights. The body shop had long campaign on human rights, highlighting abuses and increasing the global awareness of issues by making full use of the geographic advantages of their shops and supporting other human rights organizations. The last one was protect our plant. In 2001 year, huge campaign against global warming was hosted by the body shop and green peace, who advocated the use of recyclable source and materials (Adrian, P. 2012). Although profits were an essential element of long run survival in body shop and it was likely to be overall corporate and marketing objectives, but body shop seemed more to be required level of profits rather than profit that there were many other objectives, which might pursue through its pricing strategies . For example, if body shop wanted to maximize market share or simply survive, a different set of prices would be delivered than if the objectives were to maximize profits. Hence, body shop ought to see viewpoint the marketing side of pricing and it ought not to see viewpoint the production / supply side of pricing if it was a truly marketing oriented organization. The key inputs for body shop to make pricing decision whether it was marketing oriented or productive / supply oriented included production objectives or marketing objectives, demand or supply numbers were considered cost or sale price and competitors or clients consideration factors, such as beauty skin care products in competitive markets demand, i.e. To decide the price whether customers are willing and able to pay is a major consideration in the selection of pricing strategies and levels of demands . Hence, body shop ought to consider demand numbers , it ought not consider production / supply numbers if it was a truly marketing oriented organization. For example, since most of the body shop's factories were still located in the UK, where wages and salaries were much higher than in Asia, so UK itself sale product prices were higher than that from Asia itself sale product prices.

I think Body Shop was a truly marketing oriented organization more than production/supply oriented organization throughout its 30 years history. In fact, Body Shop was experiencing market level growth. It could expand its sales market in Europe, America, Middle

East, Asia and Africa etc different countries. It seemed that it had attempted to carry on marketing research to decide to choose which countries would have more client numbers to demand to buy its personal care products, then it would follow the countries' estimated client numbers to produce its products to sell to the countries. So, it was why some Asia countries sold its bath and shower and skin and hair care and colour cosmetics products more than its fragrances products, such as Hong Kong young people were more acceptable to use bath and show and color cosmetic and skin and hair care products more than fragrances products . It seemed that Hong Kong Body Shop sold fragrance products numbers were less than bath and shower and color cosmetics etc. products. Nowadays, I think the personal beauty care products new businesses which planned to entry this market was more difficult. It was possible than Body Shop was a famous personal beauty care products sale company, it had owned many clients too many years. So , it caused barriers to any new personal beauty care product competitors felt difficult to entry this market .Furthermore, Body Shop had build strong buyer and seller power to increase clients had more confident to use its products, it was possible that who felt its different kind of products could give more health to their skin or body more than other similar personal beauty care products. Moreover, I believe Body Shop had attempted to carry on technological experimenting to aim to build different countries' clients had more confident to use its products forever. In conclusion, it seemed that Body Shop was truly marketing oriented organization more than productive/ supply oriented organization oriented organization throughout its 30 years history.

Any companies need to consider the social responsibility during which are the pursuits of profit and meeting the needs of wider group of stakeholders incompatible. Without this self interest, there will be little motivation for firms to provide better services, workers couldn't earn better salaries and clients couldn't aspire for a high level of consumption. Hence, self interest which helps markets work more effectively for the benefits of all. Hence, companies should adopt a code of behavior and conduct and ethical behavior which would not influence any stakeholders groups' benefits to pursuit their profit honestly. Corporate social responsibility is a form of corporate self regulation integrated into a business model. It aims to give responsibility for corporate actions and to encourage a positive impact on the environment and stakeholders including consumers, employees, investors, communities and others and it is titled to aid an organization's mission as well as guide to what the company can give the best benefits to serve its customers. I shall use body shop company as one example to judge whether what extent are the pursuits of profit and meeting the needs of wider groups of stakeholders will be incompatible. Factually, body shop could adopt a code of behavior and conduct and ethical behavior which would not influence any stakeholders groups' benefits to pursuit their profit honestly. Such as, one of the major and most successful initiatives which body shop used an effective supply chain for their products and body shop made use of their sustainable chain supply strategy to ensure that there was the promotion and the maintenance of the social ethical behavior in its business. Hence, it seemed that body shop could be compatible to achieve an effective supply chain to deliver to different countries' stores to meet clients who had more need to buy different kinds of skin care products to provide them to choose to buy in the reasonable price choices in the short time. It is therefore in the best practices and interests for body shop to reach out to the communities in their businesses to provide raw materials to help the manufacturers of the beauty products. It also partook in the development of the market for such small scale suppliers. In many cases the body shop tried to outsource its raw materials to its customers. This had ensured the sustainability of its customer base this included it's sensitivity to its environment and the required standards of the labor practices of its partners. Hence, it seemed that body shop could be compatible to help its partners to earn profits and any countries' partners could provide more job chances to unemployed people to work from body shop's outsourcing strategy.

Hence, this had been developed by the body shop by including strategies, such as third party logistic providers and intermediaries in which who had no ownership. The body shop was a multinational company also adopted trading to purchasing approach where it shifted from short term where focus of buying articles to long term focus of fewer suppliers. This was an attempt of it to develop quality products where prices were also fair and affordable to sell to different countries' clients. It seemed that body shop could be compatible to sell reasonable prices of products to it's clients. Moreover, it had included in its strategies the aspect of business promotion using catalogues. For the same reason, it had been involved in printing of catalogues which were given out to the clients with their purchases. It was important to note that it' catalogues always contained all it's information descriptions and any person who purchased it's products was bound to receive the explanation of all it's product. This was an attempt of it to develop quality products where prices were also fair and affordable to sell to different countries' clients. It seemed that body shop could be compatible to provide clear information description in catalogues to let whose clients to know what it's different kinds of style body skin care products ingredients and benefits were , then who could compare it's products to other competitors to decide to buy or not buy fairly.

In Oct. 2007 the campaign for safe cosmetic products, in which 25 multinational companies participated, tested 33 brand name lipsticks and found one-third of the sampled exceeded the limit of lead allowed in confectionery. The affected brands included L'Oreal and Christian Dior. A definite effect would be that consumers would be more concerned regarded the ingredients of products who used, which was likely to have an effect on cosmetics and skin care products were released to capture share. It seemed body shop needed to consider its beauty personal care products were the most ensure to own organic ingredients to let any countries clients

(stakeholder) to meet their body health care needs (Adrian, P. 2012).

On the health and natural aspect, body shop had health and safe responsibility to consumers. Although, I felt who had considered this issue because it had 30 years history to operate this business and it had not received any serious negative complaints damage its health product image from clients before. However, with consumers were increasingly informed and were educated, who were now more demanding for more information regarding products and were becoming more aware of health issue. Products with organic ingredients and natural ingredients, such as tea and plants were gaining popular. Furthermore, consumers were looking for healthier substitutes to seemingly unhealthy products, such as color cosmetics. Hence, body shop began to sell the reducing numbers, it was possible due to clients compared it's body care products quality to the other competitors and who felt it's product's ingredients existed some poor ingredients to cause every one's body to be unhealthy. Hence, it's productive processing was very important. It seemed that body shop could be compatible to consider its individual client body skin health issue whether after who had used it's body skin care products to have skin hurt or skin pain feeling. In conclusion, to judge what extent are the pursuits of profit and meeting the needs of wider groups of stakeholders incompatible for any individual business, it is depended on whether the company's any stakeholders, such as employees, clients, suppliers, partners, society (communities) etc. who will have positive or negative influence from it. I feel that it will be incompatible if the company give negative influence to any one of its stakeholder. Hence, if any one company's at least one stakeholder who felt who had negative influence due to it did business to relate to whom unwillingly, then it's pursuit of profits aim would be incompatible to meet it's needs of its any one of stakeholder. Such as body shop will give positive influence to its all stakeholders. Hence, I feel it is compatible extent to pursuit of profit and meeting the needs of its wider groups of stakeholders definitely.

What are the health promotion strategy difference between Nestle company and Body Shop ?

I feel that Nestle company has managed to sustainable reconcile to pursuit profits and meeting the needs of its wider groups of stakeholders two aims compatibly. Nestle was the world's largest food and beverage company. Nestle in the United States, which represented seven operating across the USA country and it was the first expanded effort in USA and achievement tied to Nestle 's global sustainability principle and commitment. Nowadays, It served 97% of American householders and Nestle 's mission was to lead the industry in nutrition, health and wellness and to create a more sustainable future. Instead of it's mission was to pursuit of profits aim, it had also achieved specific sustainability commitment and progress in the categories of nutrition, environmental impact and water use, social impact, rural development and responsible sourcing to meet the needs of it's wider of groups of stakeholders' aim. On the nutrition, health and wellness aspect, Nestle met the needs to its stakeholder (clients), such as, Nestle rolled out new portion guidance tools and launched an educational campaign and balance your plate to help consumers build nutritious and delicious and convenient meals that met the dietary guidelines for Americans; Nestle also reduced sodium content in many of its most popular brands, such as Stouffer's and DiGiorno and committed to further reduce sodium content by 10 percent in products that did not meet the Nestle; Nestle also reduced sugar content, such as ninety six percent of Nestle 's children's products met the Nestle criteria for low sugar and by the end of 2014 year, 100 percent of children's products would meet these criteria as well as Nestle also removed trans-fat content, such as Nestle committed to reach zero food and beverage products with trans-fat originating to use as functional ingredients by 2016 year. It seemed that Nestle had considered its food and beverage production content whether these content would have negative influence to its stakeholder (clients) nowadays (Adrian, P. 2012). On the environmental impact aspect, Nestle reduced waste during it's food and beverage products were producing. As part of its commitment to eliminate all forms of waste, Nestle reduced 44 percent of waste per ton of product since 2010 year in the USA five factory locations reached zero waste to landfill status by the end of 2013 year; Nestle also considered responsible packaging responsibility, such as Nestle Waters North America led the USA bottled water industry in light weighting packaging, in part by reducing the plastic content of its 1/2 liter bottles by 60 percent since 1994 year. Since 2003 year alone, more than 3.3 billion pounds of plastic had been saved by Nestle as well as Nestle also adopted responsible sourcing, such as Nestle Purina Pet Care implemented responsible sourcing guidelines for seafood that align with Nestle 's global responsible sourcing guidelines, working with experts to track suppliers and contribute to healthier ecosystem. In 2013 year, Nestle also reached an important target for palm oil, with 100 percent of palm oil now Round table on sustainable palm oil certified. It seemed that Nestle also considerate whether environment would have negative influence occurrence during it's production (Adrian, P. 2012).

On social impact aspect, Nestle supported local communities, such as Nestle in USA donated more than $2.3 million dollars to support local United Way organizations; It also provided disaster relief, such as Nestle waters donated more than 685,000 bottled of water and Nestle Purina contributed more than 60,000 pounds of pet food and 41,000 pounds of cat little to local shelters across the USA for disaster relief as well as it grew supplier diversity, such as Nestle works with over 4,100 small, minority, women and veteran owned businesses to help to spur local economies. It seemed that Nestle also considerate social needs. Thus, it is seemed Nestle company have managed to sustainable reconcile these two aims to pursuit profit as well as it also could gave positive influence to its stakeholders. Such as consumer could feel safe to enjoy to eat Nestle company's health foods; societies could be reduced unemployment from its outsourced assistance job to partners; natural environment could be reduced pollution from its productive protection. Hence, it was not actually neglect its shareholders' benefits during it was doing business as the same time (Adrian, P. 2012).

The body shop is a global manufacturer and retailer of naturally inspired , ethically produced beauty and cosmetics products. Founded in the UK in 1976 year by Dame Anita Roddick, who now have 2,133 stores in 55 countries with a range of over 1,200 products in Europe, America, Middle East, Asia and Africa. However, the body shop has not entered the China market. It takes a strong position on activism, ethical business, human rights and environmentalism in a global perspective. The body shop is banned in China because cosmetics sold there have to be tested on animals, according to Roddick. In, 2006 when it was bought by the French cosmetics company L'Oreal which is a big player in China. China has launched scientific developing strategy for future the current policies of advocating. Hence, it is the perfect time for the body shop to enter China market. However, prior to that, as an independent member of the L'Oreal family, the body shop has to make decisions on differentiation marketing strategies, market segmentation and marketing position (Adrian, P. 2012). It might have taken two purposes to body shop marketing in its early years in order to improve its chances from short term to long term success. The short term objective was to generate more sales for the body shop. Through, the introduction of a new service, the market up class, it was hoped that clients could try and experience the body shop cosmetic products. Positive experience of using its products could then be developed through their trial using the market up class. It was estimated that this positive experience could push up the sales.

The long term objective was to educate the belief of the body shop to the young potential clients, so that who would become those who preferred natural cosmetic products and were loyal to the body shop in the future. Objectives could provide the starting point for marketing plans and strategies and should be specific targets that are obtained but also challenging. Specific, measurable, agreed, realistic and time related objectives might be taken to body shop to improve early years in chances in long term success. It seemed that Hong Kong was one good market for body shop to satisfy an unfulfilled customers needs to pursue body shop investment chance. Therefore, the objective were to push up sales and built a loyal customer basis for the future. For example, Hong Kong was one young student clients growth market to body shop. In the past, one cosmetic products market statistic was indicated that the colour cosmetic retail value had been increasing from 2002 year, HK$938.3 million dollars to 2007 year, HK$1,132,3 million dollars, so percentage was increased to 5.12% . (Adrian, P. 2012). It seemed Hong Kong might be one good skin cosmetic care products developed market to this body shop in early years. The another factor might improve body shop long term success factor was whether body shop had attempted to analyze direct competition. The body shop's direct competition was not from the name brand like Dior, Chanel or Olay, but rather the less well known brands, from Japan or Korea. Along with the great impact of Korean fashion, many Korean cosmetics brands like Missha and the Face shop had already established shops in China. These two brands also promoted their natural ingredients and target the young customer segment as what the body shop products competition concept could be offered to a market to satisfy a want or need and offered five levels, which were the core benefits, basic product, expected product, augmented product and potential product. Each level added more customer value and the five constitute client value hierarchy products of these three brands were all using natural ingredients and simple and natural in packaging. The body shop , however, differentiated itself at the top levels of the five product and transformations the products might undergo in the future.

Marketing management and planning was essential to body shop, it was the implementation of strategies to achieve long run profitability to body shop and growth. When body shop was looking at how it would achieve this in early years in order to improve the chances long term success, its two keys points to consider are: What was body shop man activity at a particular time? And how it would reach its goals? It might design a strategy that insured a consistent approach to offer its skin care products to raise competition in mind the skin care products changing market. These included product line, distribution methods, marketing communication and pricing. For example, achieving marketing research to Hong Kong and China skin care products market to analyze what were these factors to influence these country people who felt needs to buy its skin care products: Such as internal factors include personality, motivation, learning, perception and attitude; external factors included culture, social class, reference groups , family and personal influences and situational factors included time, income, mobility and availability. The reason was because due to consumers bought skin care products to protect whose skin (core benefits) and their expectations if who were willing to pay more basic product. To enhance the product level, body shop skin health product needed emphasize that skin products were natural. Products of the body shop offered the same effective and natural and flavor and unique corporate values. Body shop was mostly natural (augmented level). Far more than the visible products, the shop shop's unique corporate values create the potential value to fulfil customer's desire of making a better health world. It's good corporate desire citizenship went beyond supplying rational and emotional benefits. Body shop might enter China market to improve long term success. The body shop divided its markets to include overseas Pacific Europe, America , Australia and New Zealand, Middle East, Africa and local UK countries. Adrian, P.(2012) indicated that a sampling questionnaire survey was conducted among 200 consumers, ranging from 18 to 50 ages in May 2006, a total of 170 valid responses that were used for analysis. Among the 170 responses, 66% were females. The findings were:

(1) About 60 % hoped that cosmetics could be a symbol of being environmental friendly.

(2) 90% would choose products made of natural ingredients.

(3) 90% spent less than 300 RMB on cosmetics and skin care products quarterly.

(4) 83% Chinese youth (age range from 18 to 25 ages) were innovators and conscious of environment.

Hence, the body shop might take a share of potential market in China. It should launch its products among younger cosmetic industry were young females who chased beauty and were willing to spend money on it. So, packaging was one of the vital factors in attracting client. The body shop took a unique approach by choosing simple packaging. The package was not made for mature women. It was made for young female students, who could enjoy on international brand at an inexpensive cost. The body shop was not only to meet young people's demand for beauty , but the demand of being responsible to environment and human rights. Hence, the target market of the body shop should focus on young people ageing from 15 ages to 30 ages. Hence, body shop might take marketing research in Hong Kong and China market to have more confident to invest in these market to improve more success. Next, Whether body shop might achieve price strategy to improve to raise success chance. An assumption is when the individual client is considering the price of any a body shop's beauty skin health product. Economic theory suggests that the customer will act in a totally rational economic manner, such that body shop's every client total utility (or satisfaction) is maximized. In deciding whether try or not try body shop's product, which totally rational consumer will carefully equate whether ought to buy or ought not buy body shop's product at the asking price set will maximizing whose utility. In making judgment, the economist assumes that the consumer has perfect information about both the prices and utility of all the other competitive products in the market and that price is the only consideration in choice. Clearly there are unrealistic assumptions. Price could be determined easily when a target market was identified. (Adrian, P. 2012) From survey indicated 64% of the 170 responses spent less than 1000 RMB on cosmetics and skin care every quarter and 24% of their expenditure was between 100

RMB and 300 RMB on cosmetics an skin care. This number could not be ignored if a cosmetics company wanted to enter this large market and be a leader. For the younger generation, the prices of the products could not be high. The price of these main competitors ranges from 10RMB to 200 RMB. The prices in Hong Kong have higher than that in the USA or the UK. And the consumer's purchasing power in mainland China is much lower than that of Hong Kong . Hence, body shop should adopt a price range in China which was similar to that of the USA or the UK rather than of Hong Kong. Once the body shop established greatly reduced and the capability of price adjustment would be achieved accordingly.

Further, body shop might have chain stores selling channel strategy to attempt to achieve long term success. Sample survey revealed that supermarket was for Chinese to purchase skin care and cosmetics. 120 out of the 170 responses hoped that who could choose products from the chain stores in the future, which suggested that the body shop should build up its own stores was regarded as cares about corporate culture and corporate image. It insisted on selling in its own stores rather than setting up counters in a shopping mall. The stores of body shop could be found easily worldwide because of stores were importance in this competitive buyer. Hence, in China, its appearance should be same as worldwide. Some housewives joined the body shop as sales agent and hold sales parties for other housewives. The sales channel allowed the body shop to reach out to more clients by bringing the store directly into client's homes. This would be a totally new method of marketing in China, but it offered a good opportunity for women to choose products and share feedback in a relaxed atmosphere. This fresh concept could attract female consumers. Nowadays, students in China could only obtain famous skin care products and cosmetics brands from campus agents, as who could not afford the products sold over the counters. It was a major problem that agents could not guarantee the ingredients and the quality of the goods. If the body shop could hold small parties to share products and opinions, that would be a good way to boost sales among students. Hence, body shop might take price strategy to Hong Kong and china market to predict whether what price who could accept to raise more confident to invest to this market to improve more success. Further, body shop might also have promotion strategy to attempt to achieve long term success. The body shop adopted environmental friendly manufacturing, opposed abuses of human rights and was accountable for its actions. The unique values attracted numbers of media groups in many countries. This results in its establishing a good reputation without any advertisements. The body shop also joined numerous social causes, which substitute advertisements. In China, however, it was totally different. In this brand new market, most people were out aware of this company. If it carried on a marketing promotion of no commercials it was impossible to reach a high market share. Hence, commercial advertisements were needed in China. The body shop could use this advertisement to give on impression that women should care about their well being both mentally and physically and it had created a sexy grand with simple packaging and without objectifying women. Many brands reach customers directly by colorful commercials and show their products in movies and TV play series. For the sakes of brand image, some movies about human rights , environmental protection and animal protection could be chosen by the body shop as carriers for particular commercial as most of the audiences were well educated, well paid and environmentally concerned. The target consumers of the body shop aged from 20 to 40 ages were energetic , knowledgeable and environmentally concerned. The body shop could give some lectures on makeup or skin care on campuses to raise feeling among students. To reach brand awareness and high brand loyalty , some samples should be given to students by experience marketing approach. Hence, body shop might take promotion to Hong Kong and China schools to let many young people to know why who needed to buy skin care products to protect their body skin to persuade who felt more needs. In conclusion, the body shop was famous for creating a niche market sector for naturally inspired skin care and cosmetic products through it's unique corporate values worldwide. The significance of the body shop's early entry into China market were strongly proposed. Once the body shop decided to enter the China market, the relevant marketing strategies and management should be implemented, such as the market segmentation and market positioning with the proper consideration of Chinese consumers should be studied in order to win the mind share of potential Chinese customers with the right marketing strategies. Overall, the findings of market survey and theoretical analysis strategy support the feasibility of the body shop's early entry into China market.

Reference

Adrian, P. (2012). Introduction to marketing theory & practice, 3 rd edition, London: Oxford press.

CHAPTER TWO

Skin health product promotion methods

Skin health product promotions are used by the companies to attract customers and increase their sales. This chapter below presents to you some marketing promotion methods.

Skin Health Promotion

1. The anti-inflammatory diet (see The DeFlame Diet book)

2. Supplement options

a. Basic Health Program

b. Advanced Health Program

The term "skin health" can conjure up television commercials for various creams and lotions that are applied to the skin to make the skin healthy. In fact, most important to skin health is probably what we eat. While this may come as surprise, scientific articles discuss this relationship:

The slogan of 'Customers are the kings' is religiously followed by every business, and it is indeed the absolute truth. Where and how would businesses without customers, anyway? The marketing departments of every firm fight tooth and nail to lure customers and increase the sales of their products. Promotional methods are important and efficient marketing strategies of various companies. While millions of dollars are spent on advertising methods, promotional marketing methods are relatively less expensive and can be more effective.

Promotional marketing is a business tool that is designed to pull customers to buy the products of a company. Generally, promotional marketing is carried out by companies to launch their products or attract more potential customers. Before devising any strategy for promotional marketing, firms must ensure that they allocate a budget to the promotional marketing and set a target that gives them maximum return on the invested money.

There are basically two promotion strategies; the push strategy and the pull strategy for skin health product market. According to the push strategy, the marketers give generous discounts and benefits to the customers so that the sales can be increased drastically. This is one of the most successful strategies, and the method of giving discounts is often successful for most of the firms. The main focus here is to reduce the costs of advertising. The pull strategy, on the other hand, minimizes the use of different channels, and the major focus is on advertising the product.

Its goal is to create a potential market for the products of the firm.

Advertising is an expensive method of promotional marketing, wherein, the products are made to reach a large number of people. For example, by using electronic media, TV, radio, press and outdoor hoardings, advertisers target the audience and try to create an impact on customers. One of the oldest ways of direct promotion is to sell the products by direct interaction between the seller and buyer. It is believed to be the most difficult form of marketing, as it requires skills of persuasion and excellent communication skills.

One of the effective, popular, and preferred form of promotional methods is to arrange certain contests for the customers. We all will agree to the fact that winning surprise prizes in a shopping mall or fashion store is simply exciting. One of the most attractive marketing strategies, organizing contests among the customers is a brilliant way to promote the products.

In the quest to attract more customers, companies distribute coupons and pamphlets about the products. The customers are either given basic information about the newly launched products or they are provided with discounted coupons on the purchase of some accessories/apparels. Coupons make for an effective marketing plan for small business units.

The idea of distributing products freely sounds weird and crazy for any company, however, there is a certain element of truth in the fact that marketing firms have gained substantial promotion through the idea of free samples. While it is not logical to just distribute your products, you can devise a strategy such that the idea of free samples doesn't incur losses for your firm.

● Email marketing strategy for skin health product promotion

Email marketing strategies are helpful and applicable to the people who want their business to expand and reach out to more customers using the world wide web. Leaf through this article to know these strategies. As the number of email users increases to a whopping 1.3 billion, the sheer idea of this potential market boggles the mind of every businessman. Email advertising by far, is the cheapest mode of advertising, considering the costs involved in accessing the Internet. Working with effective strategies on the Internet can surely help businesses all around the globe to excel and make more profit. As far as understanding the technology is concerned, one doesn't have to be a web developer or software engineer for this type of marketing.

According to the Direct Marketing Association's (DMA) study and a work published by Mitchell Eisen, here are a few reasons to formulate good strategies:

Every dollar spent on email results in $46 in revenue. 43% of email recipients click the Spam button based on the email 'from' name or email address. 21% of the email recipients report email as a Spam, even if they know it isn't.

The basis of success in every business remains the same excellent marketing strategies. No matter how much a businessman spends on the operations, finance or human resource, if the marketing strategies are not good, he'll face difficulties in generating excellent revenues. Besides that, more and more people are buying products and services online and smart businessmen could profit from this fact, provided they follow good practices.

● Email marketing promotion method steps:

step 1: Look out for Targeted Customers According to the Products

The first and foremost thing before sending out emails to the prospective customers is to conduct a proper research and look out for the target group. Suppose the business is related to grocery items which can be purchased online and delivered within a city; then there is no point mailing people, if they don't reside in the same city.

step 2: Work on Catchy Subject Lines

Once the list of customers is prepared, next comes the content and subject line of the mail. An unattractive subject line will ensure that the email lands up in trash as soon as the user receives it. To tempt him to open the mail and read its content, it is very important for the subject line to be catchy. Subject lines with exclamation marks and loud words (all capital letters) usually get deleted by spam filters.

step 3: Avoid Spamming and Unethical Approaches

It is always advisable to avoid spamming and unethical approaches to reach more number of people. Spamming is illegal in over 18 states in the US, and a huge fine may be levied on people who are caught doing so. One should always try to get a genuine mailing list from trusted companies or individuals. Also, unsolicited mails shouldn't be sent to the people who have not given permission for it.

step 3: Try to Develop Good Relations with the Clients

The clients will surely keep on using the products and services, and will tend to return for the same, if good relations are maintained. It is also important because of the fact that, the customers don't see the vendor's side, and all the impression that is created, is through emails only. It also provides the benefit of 'word of mouth' publicity, in case the customer is satisfied.

step 4: Keep on Updating the Target Customers List Frequently

Keeping the list updated ensures that the customers who are not interested are omitted, and new customers are pitched. Also, the ones who show genuine interest are taken care of, from the vendor's side. New leads should be generated throughout the process of marketing in order to reach more people. Pitching more people will increase the sales and website hits for the company or an individual.

step 5: Offer Incentives to the Clients

Offering incentives and gifts ensure that the customers feel elated using the services of a particular company. Incentives like free e-books, software, or e-newspaper subscriptions can be useful for the customers. This may also increase the popularity of the company, and add to its revenues.

Besides the above listed strategies, a lot more can be done by an individual or a company itself. Marketing is a field which allows one to be creative, and this creativity is the key to form successful strategies. All the successful marketing campaigns and ideas have been accomplished by the people who tried to move beyond the conventional precincts, without forgetting the basics.

● Health & Beauty Marketing Strategy

We created The Pocket Guide to Health & Beauty Marketing to help you maximize your results. In this interactive quick read, we unpack the latest trends, research, and tips on how to make your health and beauty marketing glow.

1. Get your social strategy in order.

When it comes to health and beauty marketing, Facebook and Instagram are key players. Shoppers aren't just browsing online, they're paying attention to what their friends are doing (and products they're using), looking at influencer and brand feeds, and posting their own content at all hours of the day and night. Cult brands like Glossier are posting awesome content, including the user-generated variety, on their social channels, building especially loyal followings among both Millennials and Gen Z.

Social retargeting can be an incredibly effective way to capture more sales by helping re-engage savvy and on-the-fence health and beauty shoppers who are already engaging or are likely to engage with your brand.

Snapshot of Sephora's Instagram feed.

Dynamic retargeting ads can help. With about 1 billion monthly active users (Instagram) and 2.23 billion monthly active users (Facebook), both platforms are extremely valuable for retargeting campaigns. Re-engage shoppers that are most likely to buy with highly personalized ads and you could see a sales uplift of 12% or better.

2. Use video retargeting to bring shoppers back.

Video retargeting is a strategy you simply can't ignore. Shoppers spend a third of their time online watching video content. In particular, Gen Z streams more content (an average of 23 hours of video content a week). That's more than any other generation, not to mention nearly one full day out of every seven.

With more and more people engaging with video across all devices, video advertising is increasing 40% year-over-year and Cisco forecasts that in two years' time, more than 80% of internet traffic will be video-based. The top corner of this Glossier video from the brand's YouTube channel is a call-to-action that takes viewers directly to the Wowder product page for more information and the chance to check out.

Criteo Dynamic Retargeting generates 20-second video ads featuring a branded intro and outro, relevant product recommendations from your live catalog, and an accompanying music track – all delivered in real-time and at huge scale.
The results speak for themselves. Look at how much health and beauty retailers increased abandoned cart conversions, shopper time spent on site, and conversion rates across devices.

3. Make your mobile experiences awesome.

As our Global Commerce Review shows, more of the world shops from the palm of their hands than ever before, and app usage is growing. The latest Criteo research reveals that mobile transactions (mobile web + app) make up 65% of all transactions, and there's been a 30% YoY increase in app transactions worldwide.

In step with the mobile shopping trend, responsive design, images that read on phone screens, carts that are persistent across devices, and the ability to call up online accounts at in-store registers are becoming the norm. To meet consumers' expectations, your mobile presence needs to be optimized to capture all the on-the-go opportunities. Criteo App Retargeting allows you to advertise your beauty apps across the most common apps (including social media), making it as easy as possible for shoppers to complete their health and beauty purchases.

4. Activate data to personalize your content.

Wherever your customers are hunting around online, from mobile browsers to apps, videos and social, you need to activate as much shopper data as possible to deliver the most relevant content.

Take L'Oréal — whose subsidiaries include Lancôme, Urban Decay, Essie, NYX, Redken, Kiehl's, Biotherm, and Garnier — a category leader that uses data to personalize all the ways they connect with their shoppers at anytime, anywhere.

Criteo Shopper Graph lets you tap into three data collectives that allow you to get a fuller picture of the purchase journey, helping you reach your health and beauty customers based on factors like browsing data, shopping history, and more.
For a brand that's virtually flawless, data should be your foundation.

Omnichannel is the new normal, making a connected online and offline marketing strategy the latest must-have. Given all the ways shoppers are drowning in content, the opportunity for health and beauty brands to cut through the noise with personalized advertising across channels is limitless.

Businesses that win in the long term will have one thing in common: They'll be using data to create personalized experiences at every point in the purchase journey, from social media, to apps, on the web, and in-store.

Key Marketing Strategies for Skin Care Brands steps

Regardless of age, skin care is a very important part of taking care of your body. Skin care brands offer these days a diverse set of products to address all skin care types, concerns, and treatments. Skin care companies create many different types of formulations designed to reach a much more diverse market. There are various products for different age groups, skin types, lifestyles, and of course budgets. People of various backgrounds buy skin care products, and different markets have different needs. To successfully marketing skin care products, companies must consider these key marketing strategies for skin care brands.

For marketing skin care products successfully, brands should have a much more comprehensive strategy. The days of being able to just use print and magazine advertising are long gone. Skin care brands have to embrace Search Engine Marketing (SEM) with all the methods used to be effective online and with ecommerce websites. Some of those methods are well-known such as: Content Marketing, Search Engine Optimization, Social Media, Video Marketing, and so on.

Search engines are responsible for nearly 50% of clicks to skin care websites. Google alone accounts for almost 40% of referrals to skin care brand websites. It is simple really, 95% of consumers start their Internet experience through search. This drives skin care brands to incorporate search marketing strategies to reach these potential fans and customers. To be successful today, marketing skin care products must include a variety of tactics and strategies.

Key market strategies steps

step 1: Understanding Skin Care Market Trends and Needs

People of many different types of backgrounds shop for skin care products. Different conditions require potentially different products. For example, teenagers desire skin care products that help with acne, while more mature customers may buy products that offer more anti aging properties. Understanding the desired target market and audience is critical to establishing a successful marketing strategy. Brands that do their research or work with industry experts such as skin care business consultants have much better chances at success. Learning about the ideal customer and current trends, brands can identify how their desired audience shop, where they go online, and how to reach them. Brands that do their due diligence, avoid costly pitfalls, and reach their goals faster.

step 2 : Talking about Ingredients and the Process

Skin care customers are some of the most educated consumers. They research and take time to investigate new products, formulations, ingredients, and processes used to create skin care products. Beauty customers simply want to know how skin care products are going to improve their skin. Brands that highlight ingredients and educate the people on why certain ingredients are important for the skin treatment, have much better chances at attracting customers. Ingredients can be discussed that help customers smooth fine lines, cleanse the skin, reduce skin damage, create a healthy tone, and protect from the sun. Giving consumers the details and information they are looking for, helps brands sell product. The same accounts for the process of the formulation.

step 3: Get and Publish Customer Product Reviews

Brands should focus on getting customer product reviews and testimonials from their loyal fans and customer base to grow their market share. One of the most powerful conversion tools and marketing strategies are product reviews. Entire websites are dedicated to reviews and consumers pay attention to them. Skin care brands should have product reviews published on their websites, especially if they operate ecommerce websites. They drive sales and help with conversion. Mostly, it is expected these days by consumers and a standard in the industry. The same is true for testimonials. Some of the more powerful marketing methods are testimonial and before and after videos used by skin care brands.

Regardless of method, in Search Marketing content creation, publication, and distribution is critical to succeeding online. Skin care brands should focus a large part of their marketing strategy on online methods of marketing and advertising. Deploying Search Engine Optimization (SEO) campaigns, content marketing, Social Media Marketing, and Paid Advertising is necessary to compete and succeed as a skin care brand.

step 4: Display Visually and Give Incentives

Brands must give incentives and display them visually through key areas of the website, around shopping pages, third party sites, social media channels, via video and so forth. It is a critical motivator that must be utilized to trigger a response from the audience. Generating sales requires the creation of a variety of incentives. Those then, must be properly designed with visual appeal and displayed across all necessary channels. Companies at times create incentives, but fail to properly display them or via quality visual aids. This is a terrible mistake. Conversion rates are best when all of it is done with quality.

Brands should frequently create incentives and display them. This should change out often and there should be a variety. Brands must create incentives that are seasonal, playful, time sensitive, and so forth. Giveways are a great way to motive consumers to shop. This tactic is frequently in use these days. The more creative a brand gets the better the results usually. Working with consultants can help to gain a better understanding. Experts can quickly assist and add measurable value.

CHAPTER THREE

Successful behavioral health business development

The business development framework for provider positioning, market share, and competition has significantly shifted in the late 1990s as providers prepare for skin health market. The use of the Marketing Four Ps is a helpful tool for providers to thoroughly evaluate their product/service viability, pricing objectives, promotional mix, and place accessibility, and will allow organizations to reposition in their marketplace, maximize market share, and develop new partnerships with previous competitors.

I recommend that any skin health product manufacturers or sellers need to let their users to know that what the health care product is? Because of the current competitive environment, health care providers (hospitals, HMOs, physicians, and others) are constantly searching for better products and better means for delivering them. The health care product is often loosely defined as a service. The authors develop a more precise definition of the health care product, product line, and product mix. A bundle-of-elements concept is presented for the health care product. These conceptualizations help to address how health care providers can segment their market and position, promote, and price their products. Though the authors focus on hospitals, the concepts and procedures developed are applicable to other health care organizations.

I believe that skin health consumers will concern whether what quality level to the kind of skin health product which can bring the actual skin health function to their skin after they often use. So, quality level is one important factor to influence any kinds of skin health product sale in success. I shall indicate some promotion methods can gather users' actual feeling when they use their skin health products as below:

Survey or questionnaire method

Survey or questionnaire method is one kind of good promotion method to let any age skin health users to believe the kind of skin health product quality. The human resources needed to provide health promotion services to improve health behaviors in populations are currently limited. Health promotion and education is included in the definition of massage therapy, and many within the massage therapy profession understand that health promotion and education are a part of massage therapy practice. However, the amounts and types of health promotion activities in massage therapy practice have not been thoroughly explored.

So, when the skin health product manufacturers can make survey to enquire young people's feeling after they used its skin health products whether their feeling is good or bad. If they have bad feeling, then they need to fill their feeling to answer which aspects of its skin health products can not let them to feel its skin health function. So, participants agree or strongly agree that it is important for massage therapists to provide health promotion. Therapists with less favorable attitudes about providing health promotion reported more barriers to providing the messages to their patients. Barriers to providing health promotion included a lack of guidelines, knowledge, and skills. Training and guidelines for massage therapists regarding health promotion would be a reasonable next step for future research development. Utilizing massage therapists as health promoters may provide opportunities to deliver more prevention messages to patients which may impact public health. So, survey method can help any skin health product manufacturers may know whether which aspects of its skin health product quality is needed to improve in order to raise their users' satisfactory feeling more easily.

TV or magazine advertisement

In skin health product market, if one skin health product brand can bring its skin health can let its users to absorb more nutrition and keep more younger age feeling after they use its skin health products. Then it will persuade them to choose its skin health product more than other kinds of similar skin health protection function products in preference in this skin health production product sale market.

The question is : How to let its skin health protection product users to believe its products have the actual young age keeping and absorbing nutrition function ? So, choosing the most suitable advertisement or promotion method, it is the important factor to achieve this aim in success. However, any kinds of skin health advertisement, they must need to let their users to believe their skin health products have these skin health functions as below:

Nutritional protection against skin damage from sunlight.

Firstly, the brand of skin health product must need to let users to feel its products have this essential function. Nutritional protection against skin damage from sunlight. The concept of systemic photoprotection by dietary means is gaining momentum. Skin is continuously exposed to ultraviolet (UV) radiation, the major cause of skin disorders such as sunburn, photodamage, and nonmelanoma skin cancer. Most of the erythemal annual UV dose is encountered under nonvacation conditions, when no sunscreen is applied. In the absence of topically added compounds, skin protection depends solely on endogenous defense. Micronutrients can act as UV absorbers, as antioxidants, or can modulate signaling pathways elicited upon UV exposure. UV-induced erythema is a suitable parameter to assess photoprotection. Dietary protection is provided by carotenoids, tocopherols, ascorbate, flavonoids, or n-3 fatty acids, contributing to maintenance resistance as part of lifelong protection.

Discovering the link between nutrition and skin health aging

Secondly, skin has been reported to reflect the general inner-health status and aging. Nutrition and its reflection on skin has always been an interesting topic for scientists and physicians throughout the centuries worldwide. Vitamins, carotenoids, tocopherols, flavonoids and a variety of plant extracts have been reported to possess potent anti-oxidant properties and have been widely used in the skin care industry either as topically applied agents or oral supplements in an attempt to prolong youthful skin appearance. This review will provide an overview of the current literature "linking" nutrition with skin aging.

Face reading technology and video camera recording promotion method

The impact of emotions on judges, evaluations and decisions have long been important to psychology and consumer behavior on consumption. I shall examine how distinct perspectives shape the processes of appraisal that lead to emotional experience and how different consumers might define happiness distinctly. I examine emotions that vary by positive, negative and mixed. I also suggest new ways to distinguish among emotions and to assess how new ways to consumers to aim to be discovered by better understanding how consumers manage their experience of emotion to achieve their own affective goals. Recording any skin health product users their face skin appearances after they uses the kind of skin health product for a long time , e.g. one year. So, the skin health product manufacturer can observe whether its skin health users whose face skin changes are more health or not.

● Main Problem Being Addressed of face reading and video camera technology limits

Technologies that detect skin health users' face skins, it can help companies to reduce the amount of money waste on unsuccessful product launches by stopping products before they are launched. Methods can be accurately measured their skin health users' feelings irrespective of consumer's ability to accurately articulate those feelings . These methods will be based on the measurement of human physiology-most likely facial expressions, but they reveal intentionally hidden or subconscious emotions. In addition, the method may be able to decide emotions: Such as happiness, sadness, surprise, fear, anger feeling when one youth person uses the kind of skin health product for long time. The first aspect main problem concerns how face reading technology can be measured to predict the skin health user acceptance level of face skin health feeling from their face expression in the short time more absolutely. However, this face reading technology can't be used to predict any skin health individual enjoyable acceptance satisfactory level when who uses any face skin health manufacturer's products in the short time.So face reading technology can not be used to predict any face skin health users' emotion to reflect to use any face skin health product quality more easily. Thus, I shall recommend how to use video camera recording ethnographic research method to find what factors to influence the face skin health user who decides to buy the kind of face skin health product to use and evaluate whose satisfactory level to use the product at home. I concern how to use video camera to predict consumer individual behavioral process to find why who choose to buy the kind of face skin health product to evaluate the most absolute emotion response to find whether who satisfies or doesn't satisfy to use the product.

● Summary of ethnographic research
of facial reading technology and video camera technology

To detect the kind of face skin health user's emotion whether who enjoy or does not enjoy to use the manufacturer's face skin health product and to find what factor(s)can influence the consumer to choose to buy the product. For example, the home product manufacturer may use digital cameras and computer recording method to record the volunteer daily routines filmed at home. It aims to detect consumer's individual using behavior to research whether what psychological factors are to influence who to choose to buy the manufacturer's product to use. Otherwise, Ethnographic research concerns how to use video camera to record consumers' behavior daily about one weeks. It aims to predict what factors case who to buy the kind of product. Hence, any face skin health manufacturers can use face reading technology to predict consumer emotion of satisfactory level to use themselves kinds of face skin health products. Home product manufacturers can use video camera technology to predict consumer emotion of satisfactory level to use products at home e.g. clothing, radios, televisions, furniture, sleeping beds etc. home daily useful products.

● Recommendation Ethnographic consumer behavior research is for video camera recording to face skin health users' facial use daily behavior at home

Otherwise, it seems any face skin health product manufacturers can't use face reading technology to detect face skin health consumers' emotion in the short time immediately. The products include any kind of products, e.g. high technological products, such as space mining of resources machines, satellite navigation system ,cars , machines etc. as well as home useful technological electronic products, such as mobile phones, washing machines, televisions, laptops as well as daily products, such as shirts, shoes, furniture, toys, tooth pastes etc. These essential home product and high technologic product manufacturers who need to continue to innovate their old style products to follow consumers' taste to invent new style products to be accepted to their fresh taste. It seems that any kinds of skin health product manufacturers need to spend a long time to touch face skin health consumers' feeling whether whose old style technological products which are still accepted to them to use or not. Hence, it implies that a face skin health consumer decides to buy these high technological innovation products, whose choice isn't performed to show who must accept to use the kind or brand of face skin health products for long time, whose emotion is not sure whether who feels satisfactory to to use this kind of face skin health product for a long time. When he/she uses this kind of face skin health product for a long time, it is possible that who will feel it was not valuable to buy it before. Hence, video camera can used to record the face skin health consumer's behavior record whose image and to analyze whose facial expressions and bodily gestures at home about one week.

● How to use video camera recording to predict face skin health product consumer's emotion .

How to use automated facial expression analysis for emotion and behavior prediction. The expression of emotion is achieved through combinations of verbal and nonverbal information produced from various sources of the body and the brains. Nonverbal information encompasses any message that is not expressed in words, including gestures, postures to be performed from individual behavior for individual daily life. Though people often don't invest much thought to the nonverbal aspect of communication to be performed to manage emotional experiences. Computers enable researchers to process to gather data in a short amount of time to predict facial expression consumers. The new methodological for social scientists may be a valid analysis to automated facial expression from consumer's daily behavior at home experiment for several days investigation more absolutely. Among the various models of nonverbal communication, we focus on facial expression which are captured by small digital cameras and later analyzed with computer software. As Webb et. al. (2000) pointed out, "people are low-fidelity observational instruments recording and interpretation may be erratic over time, as the observer learns and responds to the research phenomena he or she observes. It means that we can observe consumer behavior to predict why who buy the product from whose daily life behavior performance. Recent studies applied automated feature extraction and classification to extract macro features . Such as the head and hand position and angle from video features taken during an experiment where a theft took place. It also implied that computer models obtained up to 71 percent correct classification of innocent or guilty participants based on the macro features extracted from the video camera. Furthermore, in an overview of detection research." Meservy et al.(2008) noted that "the accuracy of humans coding behavioral indicators only falls around 50 percent, but that computers trained to a automatically extract and identify relevant behavioral cues detect deception with significantly higher accuracy. Furthermore, computers operate without the other methods(e.g. physiological measures such as polygraph machines or lie detectors) and the lost of extensively trained human interviewers." Ambady and Rosenthal (1992) showed that "another advantage of why automated facial detection technology coupled with computational models is that once the system secures the parameters for a model, prediction of behavior (vs simple detection and classification) can be made using only a small sample. This is a computational recording of what social psychologists, a way people sample a short except from social behavior to draw inferences of about states, traits and other personally relevant characteristics .For instance, based on an observation of a three minute video clip of a conflict between a married couple." Carrere and Gottman(1999) also indicated "video cameras were able to predict the outcome of that marriage after six years.

Using machine learning coupled with computer vision allows computers to cause this human cognitive process; models are trained on a short sample of facial features and those features automatically predict future behaviors. Computers were used in place of human coders to detect vocal behaviors (e.g. time spent speaking, influence over conversation partners, variation in pitch and volume and behavior mirroring) during a negotiation task. Their results imply that the speech features extracted during the first five minutes of negotiation are highly predictive of future outcomes." The researchers also noted that using computers to code speech features offers advantages such as high test-retest reliability and real time feedback. As a cost-effective and relatively accurate method to detect, track and create models for behavior classification and prediction, automatic facial expression analysis has the potential to be applied to multiple disciplines. Capturing behavioral data from participants may be a more accurate representation of how and what they feel, and a better alternative to self-report questionnaires that interrupt participants' affective cognitive processes and are subject to bias .Our model goes beyond to predict the future behavior within a given task (e.g. a virtual car accident or an error in performance). This opens up the possibility of such models becoming a common methodology in social scientific and behavioral research.

Installing video camera recording at sample face skin health consumers to carry on investigating their feeling to use the kind of face skin health product to collect the more truly acceptable or not acceptable feeling to use the product reason, such as: video camera recording method is data synchronization and time series statistics calculation. In the next phase of analysis, video recording are recording with data collected from experimental tasks such as surveys or simple motor tasks. This is done to map the extracted facial geometry information to behavioral output data. In the experiments three to five second intervals of facial expressions were taken one to two seconds before each instance of the behavior to be predicted and used as the input data. After data synchronization we also computed a series of time-domain statistics on coordinates in each interval to use as additional inputs to our classifiers. For example one sample investigating. The input data for this study consisted of videotapes of forty one participants watching films that elicited the emotions of either amusement or sadness, along with measures of their cardiovascular activity responding. It should be noted that the recorded expressions were expressions, unlike the photographs of deliberately posed faces often used in prior facial expression research. However, I suggest these entertainment product or home product manufacturers who can use video cameras to record whose buyers' behavior to detect whose emotion to aim to design which kind of colors, styles, sizes and how to change whose old products' features to attract the more consumers' fresh demand taste .

Ethnographic research is interpretative research which seeks an understanding from the perspectives of the value systems of those being researched. Ethnographic search is one different method to learn about buyer individual behavior to compare with enquiring questionnaires to participants to fill to answer questions to gather data to carry on the sale and post purchase evaluation cycle to evaluate whether what are their product criteria or weaknesses which need to improve to raise their sale competition in their market. Palmer (2012) reported " one sport shoe company's ethnographic research in action was provided by a product commissioned by the footwear brand Dr Martens. It aims to research how to understand young people's buying behavior. It wanted to understand how youth people used brands in their every lives. Why for example, did some brands , such as Nike trainers or baseball caps become popular in youth culture? The researchers identified groups of young people around the world who responded to Dr Marten's target market. In return for a payment, volunteers were followed for several days and their daily routines filmed with a handheld digital camera. In total, 180 hours of captured film was edited to just one hour of highlights showing the key drivers of youth culture which are relevant to the Dr Martens brand. It seems that young people preferred fashions that allowed them to customize an item of clothing and in some way take ownership of it. The research drew the conclusion that iconic fashion items for young people had to have a distinctive label or style that made their wearers stand out as part of a tribe." Hence, ethnographic research seems to help this company to know why the young clients choose to buy those brands sport shoes, it is possible that the these brands sport shoes' color or design can be accepted more to them to buy Dr Marten brand's sport shoes when they wear different style of clothing. Hence, it uses digital cameras to observe the worldwide choice of paying target youth volunteers whose daily individual behaviors at homes to get the more actual evidence to evaluate what factors influence youth clients choose to buy these brands of sport shoes. It seems this sport shoe company can take several hours of filming to yield just a few moments of true insights to participant's true attitudes and behavior. Ethnography is one of many approaches that can be found within Social research. Ethnography was a descriptive account of a commonly or culture. Ethnography usually involves the researcher participating in people's daily lives for an extended period of time, watching what happens, listening to what is said, and/or asking questions through informal and formal interviews collecting documents. In more detailed terms, ethnographic work usually has most of the following features: People actions are studied in every contexts rather than under conditions created by the researcher, in experimental or high structured interview situations as well as data are gathered for a range of sources including documentary evidence of various kinds, but participant observation and/or relatively informal conversations are main ones as well as data collected is for the most past relatively unstructured in two senses and it doesn't involve following through detailed research design at the start and the categories that are used for interpreting what people say or are not built into the data collection process through the use of observation schedules or questionnaires to analyze. Generally, fairly small scale perhaps a style setting or group of people.

This is a facilitate in depth study and analysis of data involves interpretation of the meaning, functions and consequences of human actions and low are implicated in local and perhaps also wider contexts what are produced for the most part are verbal descriptions, explaining and theories and statistical analysis play a subordinate role at most. How ethnography can learn more about buyer behavior to help product manufacturers to detect consumers' emotion. It means collection of data to pursue an answers to these questions more effectively and to test those against evidence. Hence, video camera recording to consumer's individual useful behavior at whose home. It isn't set up for research purposes (such as experiments or formal interviews). The methodological model for social research is physical science conceived in terms of the logic of the experiment. However, ethnography was sometimes dismissed as quite inappropriate to social science on the grounds that data and findings it produces are subjective. Hence, ethnographic research is the role to learn more about buyer behavior through marketers may have been listening more to consumers (e.g. through qualitative research), efforts have almost always been directed at controlling consumers ranges of products or services predetermined by producers have been pushed through with littler real involvement of consumers in the process at a time in which consumers are ever more aware of what is being done to marketers. To seeing any kind or brand of face skin health consumer's daily life behavior can predict why who choose to buy your or your competitor's product. Then, the face skin health product manufacturer can judge what the reasons are caused to attract the consumer chooses to buy the product to use. Hence, the data analysis procedure will include these steps as below:

● First step, Facial expression videos camera record activity ; input data from given tasks will be carrying on researching at the same time.

● Second step, the feature extraction will be caused

● Third step, the chi-square feature selection will be caused

● Fourth step, the machine learning training will be caused

● The final step, the results of behavioral prediction and data classification will be output at the same time.

● Why ethnographic research can be predicted consumer's behavioral performance to detect emotion by video recording camera at home ?

Ethnographic field research involved the study of groups and people as go about every day lives. There has two distinct activities. First the ethnographer enter into a social setting and gets to know the people and observes all the approach. But second the ethnographer writes down regular systematic ways what who observes and learns when participating in the quality rounds of life of others. Thus, the researcher creates an accumulating written records of these observations and experiences. Two interconnected activities comprise the care of ethnographic search: participation in some initially familiar social world and the production of written accounts of that world by drawing upon such participation. Hence, ethnographers are committed to get close to the activities and everyday people. Getting close minimally requires physical and social proximity to the daily rounds of people lives and activities, the field researcher must be able to take up positions in order observe and understand whom.

Consumer behavior refers to the behavior that consumers display in searching for purchasing , using , evaluating and disposing of products and services that who expect will satisfy their needs and it's behaviors that are directly involved in the action of obtaining, consuming and spending products or services, including the decision processes that precede and follow these actions. It seems ethnographic research can helps the marketer to understand how consumer think, feel and select from alternative like products, brands and the like and how the consumers' buying behaviors are influenced by their environment, the reference group, family and salespersons. Consumer buying behavior includes that: Attitude itself is a learning experience and can lead to a change in attitude before buyers enter the buying process. Thus, attitude don't automatically guarantee all types of behavior. Attitudes based on behavioral learning follow beliefs, behaviors and effect sequence. A consumer who is high involved with a product or service category and who perceives a high level of product or service differentiation between alternatives with follow the cognitive hierarchy (belief affect behavior). From the ethnographic research marketers perspective the sequence of attitude formation is from a communication point of views from a strategic point of view, such as it has proved useful in specifying the different elements that work to influence buyers' evaluations of attitude, product or services may be composed of attributes or qualities, some of which may be more important than others to particular people. So consumer's individual decision is to act on whose attitudes is affected by other factors, such as whether it is felt other factors, such as whether it is felt that buying a product or service would be met with approval by friends and family.

According to this approach, ethnographic research marketers must concentrate an assessing the characteristics of the environment, such as the physical surroundings and product or service placement, that influence members of that target market. Such as point of purchase (such as selling the sport shoe brand's some sample of design style shoes) are particularly useful in predicting to find reasons why individual consumer choose to buy these styles. Hence, I recommend ethnographic research marketers can focus on measuring consumers' effective emotion response to products or services and develop offering that elicit appropriate subjective reactions and employ effective symbolism to predict how the different brand products to be designed which kind of style, to be used what kinds of colors and what kinds of materials to be produced. To decide which is the most acceptance to satisfy consumers' taste. Such as the above sport shoe brand company case showed that it attempted to use ethnographic method to research whether what the external or internal factors are influenced to the footwear brand Dr martens' other consumers to choose the Nike or Baseball brands sport shoes to buy. It discovered that what youth people whose daily wearing clothing colors, designs and materials external factors which can influence them to choose to buy which kinds of design styles, colors and materials made of sport shoes to buy. It seems famous brands of sport shoes and cheaper price and durability internal factors are not the important factors to influence them to choose to buy these brands. Otherwise, the youth people whose wearing clothing colors, design styles and material made external factors can influence their feeling to choose the most adaptable style of sport shoes to be accepted to adapt to accept to their wearing clothing fashion. Thus, it seems that ethnographic research is one good method to detect consumers emotion whether the individual consumer's choice is influenced by the product's internal factors more or external environment external factors more to influence every individual consumer to feel positive or negative emotion to make final decision to buy any product to use possibly. If the product manufacturer can use this ethnographic research method to attempt to find whether what external or internal factors can influence potential consumers' fashion acceptance level to choose to buy any new innovative products to predict their emotion before the new product manufacturer decides to manufacture its products to sell in this competitive market. I believe that its predicting market success chance will be increased to any kind or brand of face skin health product manufactuers.

How to evaluate online sale method is more acceptable to sell the kind of face skin health product

● Abstract

The third aspect solution, I shall explain why the electronic commerce sale channel in technology acceptance model, it is possible that why it can influence the face skin health consumer's positive emotion to be changed to be negative emotion to choose not to buy the manufacturer's product . Moreover, I shall teach manufacturer whether how to judge it ought or does not ought choose this technology model to sell its products from internet channel.

● Main Problem Being Addressed

The third aspect main problem is researched why internet sale will have what bad factors to influence face skin health consumers to cause negative emotion to decide not to buy manufacturers' products from online shopping. I shall recommend how to predict their products whether which are suitable to sell from internet and how to improve their sale methods to increase consumer's positive emotion to accept to buy their products from internet. The final discussion is judged in what situation it will cause individual consumer doesn't like to enter the manufacturer's website to choose to buy the manufacturer's products.

I shall also indicate why the manufacturer will cause negative emotion to whose consumers if who chose online sale channel. I aim to teach manufacturer how to know whether whose products ought or not ought to be chose to sell from online sale channel as well as how to reduce to cause bad influence to consumers' emotion from whose websites to avoid online sale failure chance. I shall use internet surveys to gather information to detect whether what factors influence the consumer choose prefer to buy or not to prefer buy the manufacturer's products from internet as well as how manufacturers can predict consumer's emotion in the constructive consumer choice process before who choose online shopping. Hence, if the manufacturer could predict whether what weaknesses are existed to reduce whose website attraction to whose consumers' attention. It will avoid whose online sale failure. The benefits to manufacturer include who can predict what weaknesses of whose website are, then who can attempt to revise which aspects of whose website weaknesses in order to raise whose consumers' positive emotion when who uses internet to enter the sale website to find any kinds of products to buy them. If the manufacturer's website can raise attraction ability to increase many customers to see whose website. Then, the kind or brand of face skin health customer numbers will be increased possibly. Online sale influence research can only apply to manufacturers who sell their products from their website sale channel.

● Related Background of internet sale channel

Nowadays, many young people like to choose to use internet to buy any manufacturer's products. Although internet is popular to accept to young to use to buy any products, but it will have chance to cause negative emotion to individual consumers from positive emotion due to they enter any manufacturer's website to find some bad points to influence their feeling to be bad. Finally, the consumers will not choose to buy the manufacturer's products due to the manufacturer does not know what the bad points are existed to whose website. Thus, I believe that internet won't be accepted to be the best sale channel to adopt to use to sell to any manufacturers' products effectively, even internet sale channel will cause some consumers negative emotion to influence who choose not to buy the manufacturer's products if the kind of face skin health product's manufacturer chooses internet to help who to advertise whose this product to sell from internet sale channel.

Previous research has linked the experience of loneliness with materialism, suggesting that when consumers attach too great an importance to possessions, they may reduce the importance of their social relationships, leading to isolation and feelings of loneliness. Thus materialism may arises a way to cope with loneliness, which suggests that to decrease materialism, one may want to first focus on building social relationships and reducing loneliness rather than focusing first upon reduced consumption. Hung & Mukhopadhyay (2012) examined the influence of actor versus observes perspectives on the emotional experience. "They find that "actors tend to focus move on the situation at hand and experience more emotion, such as excitement, sadness when who recall or anticipate emotional experiences. Their previous research has linked experiences of loneliness with materialism, suggesting that when consumers attach to great an importance of their social relationship, leading to isolation and feelings loneliness. This may unfortunately, lead to downward, thus it focus on building social relationship and reducing loneliness rather than focusing first upon reduced consumption." It seems social environment can influence the consumer's social emotion to choose to consume the product. The meaning of happiness that is most relevant to influence choices, such select those with a present focus will prefer products that offer calm. Thus, it seems excited consumers will choose exciting products and calm consumers will choose relaxing products. It implies that who will prefer to choose to buy the kind of product from online shopping if the consumer is a excited person to accept new technology shopping model and enjoyed to loneliness to sit down to use whose laptop to choose to buy any online products at home quiet environment. Otherwise, if consumers don't like loneliness, who will like to leave their homes to go to retail shops to buy any manufacturers' new innovate products with their friends or families and who will feel more happy and enjoyable in this non technological shopping model. Thus, it implies the enjoyable quiet environment, loneliness, technology excited consumers will choose to buy products from online sale model more. Otherwise, the enjoyable noise environment, social relationship, calm consumers will choose to buy products from traditional retail shops sale channel. Thus, consumers' emotion will be influenced to feel enjoyable or non-enjoyable to buy the product from the online shopping model or traditional visiting retail shops model .It seems that noise or quiet shopping environment will influence individual consumer's emotion to make final decision to buy the product. If the consumer enjoys to choose to buy any brands of products in the quiet environment at home lonely, the online shopping technological model will be more chance to be accepted to make final decision to this consumer habitually. Otherwise, if the consumer enjoys to choose to buy any brands of products in the noise environment, social relationship with friends, the visiting retail shops model will be more chance to be accepted to make final decision to this consumer habitually. What is this meaning to this consumer in these two different situation? I feel that the consumer will prefer to choose to buy the kind of product from online shopping if who is a excited person, so who can accept to use internet more than visiting retail shops , due to who enjoys to loneliness to sit down to use whose laptop to choose to buy any online products at home quiet environment. Otherwise, if the consumer does not like loneliness, who will like to leave whose home to visit retail shops to choose to buy any brands of products with whose friends or families in the noise shopping center environment, due to who will feel more happy and enjoyable to buy any products in the noise and social relationship with friends or family outside environment. It means that the product manufacturer needs to understand whether whose products can be more accepted to sell to its potential consumers from either online sale model or visiting retail shops traditional sale model as well as how to design its product styles to match its potential consumers to build positive emotion whether this product is suitable to sell from online sale channel. In general, the perceived case of use can influence perceived usefulness of the product, then to influence consumer's attitude to choose to buy the product. Hence, attitude can influence the consumer's commonly. I feel that the consumer will choose to visit retail shops to test the product's functions or attempt to touch the product or see the product's actual image in the retail shops, even who needs the salespeople to teach who how to use the product when feel the product is difficult to learn to use. Specially, it is a new innovative technological product, when it will be promoted to market to sell in the first time. Due to the consumer did not know this new product existed before, who needs the salespeople talk to whom to explain how to use this new technological innovative product to listen carefully. So, who will choose to visit retail shops to decide to buy this product with whose friends or families more than online shopping. Otherwise, if the consumer feels the product is ease to use and who like loneliness, who will accept to use internet to make final decision to choose online to buy the product in the quiet home environment more than traditional visiting retail shops model. It seems the external environment and the consumer's personality can influence the consumer's emotion to make final decision to choose to buy any brand of product. For example, the consumer feels the product is ease to learn to use or difficult to learn to use. It will influence the consumer choose to buy either from online or retail shops.

● How can internet cause positive emotion to face skin health consumers?

Online shopping lacks emotion physically experienced (e.g. examined, tried on, and used), it is difficultly for shoppers with little computer expertise, there are some general uncertainties associated in homes hopping of all kinds (e.g. concerns about product return, credit card security, loss of privacy, merchant legitimacy.) Each consumer's confidence might play an important role in predicting intentions to purchase. The factors influence whose confidence which may include, such as consumer's lower perceived risk, product appearance, image size and product movement were manipulated in context of simulated appeal web sites. Both manipulations in the computer medicated environment were expected to create virtual experiences affecting mood, perceived risk and purchase intent product image size is a significant factor. Product presentations using movement attract attention and generate good mood in on-line shoppers, even soft music listening in quiet home environment can influence consumer's emotion to cause online shopping intention. The benefits of online shopping in relation to traditional stores hopping are one of the driving forces in the adoption. Perceived usefulness has been used to explain consumer acceptance of online shopping. Perceived usefulness refers to the degree to which a person believes that using a particular system (e.g. an online shopping site) would enhance his or her job performance. Risk perception of online shopping can be risked into two predominant types behavioral risk and environment risk. Behavioral risk arises from online retailers who have a chance to behave in an opportunistic manner by taking advantage of the government's inability to monitor all transactions adequately. It includes product risks, psychology risks and seller performance risks. Environment risk is caused by the unpredictable nature of the purchasing medium-internet, which is beyond the control of online retailer and consumer. It includes financial risks and privacy risks. Perceived risk can be affected or moderated by a variety of factors, including consumer demographics, internet experience, product characteristics and attributes of a web site etc. The perceived product risk varies with the age and internet experience of consumers. As consumers get older, their accumulated experience and knowledge make their stopping more targeted of certain brands and make them more confident, which can reduce product risk and the need for conducting pre-product information searches. It is possible that in comparison to make consumers female consumers perceived the likelihood and consequences of negative outcomes as a result of purchasing online to be greater and their concerns regarding these verity of the consequences of privacy loss during online shopping were stronger. The effect of perceived risk may be subject to product characteristics. The risk is generally higher for high involvement products that require the problem solving behavior and have some degree of personal importance than for low involvement products. Hence, online retailers of low involvement products may have greater success in keeping buyers than those of high involvement products, if the former can provide on appealing shopping experience. Other attributes of products do matter to perceived risk . For example, the risk was perceived lower for product for categories associated with higher expenditure levels, more satisfying characteristics and feeling and touching before purchase. Consumer attitude is directly affected by users' belief about a system, which consist of perceived usefulness and once of use to use online to shopping in technology acceptance model to each individual consumer. In the technological acceptance model aspect view, it is possible that the consumer's perception of technology of safety and cost is important to influence who to choose to buy the product as well as self efficiency has been found to affect technology usage also through its effects on the emotional state of the user buy, for example, the manufacturer can reduce the consumer whose computer anxiety and it can increase behavioral control to its consumer more easily when its consumers enter it's product website to feel it is more safe to buy its products to compare to its online competitors' websites. Due to the characteristics of online retail context to innovative products, consumers are subjected to more influences in the virtual store where who are able to interact with an adaptive environment as a consequence on adaptive and interactive scenario is more appealing for consumers, with benefits for the decision making process. Thus, internet will influence consumers whose emotion to choose another online shopping model to any innovative products sale channel. Enjoyment can be considered the degree to which consumer perceives a certain technology as pleasant. It implies that richer technology leads to higher enjoyment for achieving a stronger influence on consumers' attitudes toward online retailers. I shall recommend any one innovative product manufacturer ought send questionnaires by to any individual consumer by email to enquire about such as below:

(i) Do you feel this kind of innovative product is either easy or difficult more to learn to use ? It aims to predict their emotion to give feedback to let who to know whether consumers' emotion will be felt more easy or more difficult to use this product from these sample population. Then , this manufacturer can judge whether it ought to sell this kind of innovative product from either traditional retail shops or online shopping model.

(ii) Do you feel you like to buy this kind or brand of face skin health product in either quiet environment or noise environment more? It aims to predict their positive emotion response to judge whether who accept to buy this kinds of innovative product in the quiet environment or noise environment more to decide to make visiting retail stores channel or online sale online to sell this product.

(iii) Do you like to use internet advertisement or magazine advertisement channel to find this kind of face skin health product? It aims to predict internet online sale model or retail stores sale channel which is more acceptable to sell the manufacturer's products to attract to influence many customers to make final decision to buy its products more popular and acceptable.

(iv) Do you need face skin health salespeople to talk to you to give truly products information to assist you to buy my brand of any products? .absolutely need .absolutely not need .may be need. may not be need. It aims to judge whether the online sale is more important sale channel or not to compare with retail shops sale channel. After it gathers these statistic information from these sample potential Consumers' email questionnaires, the manufacturer can analyze whether this kind of innovate product is more acceptable from online sale model or traditional retail shopping model in its country, even global sale. Thus, it can decide either to increase to open more retail shops or decrease retail shops numbers or concentrating on selling its products from online sale channel more sale methods.

Consumer emotion prediction can have many methods. However, I feel that these three methods are the most useful. Firstly, video camera recording technology can predict why the consumer chooses to buy the kind of product as well as face reading technology can measure whether what weights of the sugar ingredients to manufacture the weight of sweets, chocolate, soft drinks of the most good taste foods. Secondly, the manufacturer can concentrate on manufacturing whose new product which can own the most attractive attributable factor to attract which customers to choose to buy to reduce the invent lose risk. Thirdly, website sale channel must not be suitable to any manufacturers to choose to sell which products. If who can know whether their products are suitable to sell from internet or retail stores sale channel more. It can reduce the risk to loss their customers in long time.

However, if you feel your product or food ought to sell from online channel. I recommend you ought need to do marketing research to evaluate whether which sale channel is the most suitable to research to sell your products or foods to persuade your clients to choose to buy. Otherwise, if your online sale channel is not suitable to sell to cause bad emotion to your clients. Thus, I believe it will reduce your client numbers due to you sell your products in the wrong sale channel. In conclusion, online sale prediction method, face emotion reading prediction method and client choice process prediction method can be attempted to test any kind or brand of face skin health product respond to predict how to raise product attraction by any face skin health manufacturers nowadays.

References

Ambady, N. and Rosenthal, R.(1992)' Thin Silces Of Behavior As Predictors Of Interpersonal Consequences: A meta- analysis, psychological Bulletin, 2: 256-74

Arnade, E. (2014) Journal Of Consumer Research, Make a face: Implict and explict measurement of facial expression by orange juices using face reading technology. Food http://hdl.handle.net/10919/54538.

Carrere, S. and Gottman, J. (1999) ' predicting divorce

amongnewlyweds from the first three minutes of a marital conflice discussion', family processes 38:293-301.

Hung & Mukhopadhyay.(June 2012), Emotion And Consumer Behavior, , vol. 40 no.5 (June 2012), 39-50.

Meservy, T.O. jnsen, M.L. Kruse, W.J., Burgoo, J.K. and Nunamaker Jr., J.F. (2008) ' Automatic extraction of deceptive behavioral cues from video', in H.Chen, E. Reid, J. Sinai, A. Silke and B. Ganor (eds) Terrorism Informatics (pp. 495-516), New York: Springer.

Miller, K. (2012), Consumer behavior, Washington, USA. Retrieved: http://www.amazon.com

Palmer (2012), Consumer behavior and credit card payment, Journal of management market resarch.

Webb et. al (2000), The impact of perceived corporate social responsibility on consumer behavior, Journal of business research 59(1): pp. 46-53 Jan. 2006.

Advertisement how influences face skin health product consumer behavior

In the globalization , improvement of technology, science, society, economy and education provide people to with better standard of living and styles. Relating to the development of purchasing power in consumers and market trend that people become more conscious of hygiene and beauty [1], it affects to the rapid growth in beauty care industry, especially in this decade. Cosmetics market in the world, especially the professional skin care has emerged stronger thanks to the increasing demand of customers, especially for the skin care brand, health sector development strongly grew in 2011. Most of people would like to be beautiful, healthy and good looking. There is a normal fact that most people want to look like the models. Men and women are alike, a smooth and bright skin with an ideal body shape for a wonderful life . Not only women need beauty care, men should be increasingly cared more for themselves. Today, with the unpredictable changes of weather, everyone needs a cosmetic capable of protecting their skin to avoid the impact of the environment. Especially men, who are exposed to harsh external environment frequently, the more necessary the use of cosmetic skin care. The beauty industry for women has been obviously growing since long times ago whereas the men's market have just become blooming in men aspects lately. In recent years, Vietnam is heavily influenced by trends of beauty in the world, the concept of male beauty has gradually changed. Currently men are more aware of their body and the demand for beautifulness, aesthetics, youthfulness, healthiness, and thinness which drag them away from old opinion about "only sanitation". Men pay more attention to their appearance, are more interested in cosmetics.

How and why advertisement can influence or persuade skin health product users to feel urgent use need. For example, when one traveller plan to travel, when he turns on television to see one brand skin health product advertisement to let him to know this brand's face skin health product how brings skin health advantage to him when he is travelling to another country. So, he will be influenced to buy this brand of skin health product in preference, when he needs to go to beach to swim or climb on mountain in his journey. So, this TV advertisement may persuade him to choose to buy this skin health brand product if he needs to do any kinds of sport in sunshine outdoor environment in his travelling journey. In services require time (holiday, travel, etc.), decisions are forming important part of consumer behaviour. One notice thing is that purchase decision does not finish with purchase of goods or services, but also post purchase activities are consisted of consumer behavior.

However, if this brand of skin health product can bring this positive message to let any sport TV audiences to know, then it can increase its attraction to persuade them to choose to buy its brand of skin health products more easily. The message may include:

(1) The TV advertisment may brings positive health body message after the skin health product users choose to buy its brand skin health product, when the users are staying in air or water pollution environment. Skin's Health Attention The skin can tell a lot about

your health. If you pay more attention, it can be a dominant early-warning system for a range of concerns about health problems . Male are typically out in the factors more than female, their skin are more affected by UV rays, environmental pollution, wind damage, and other factors that all work together to harm the skin, creating more wrinkles and hyperpigmentation. First, men need to be cared about their health. Men can be using sunscreen, in addition, they need moisturizers that are fulfilled with protective antioxidants. Protection against skin cancer is the best reason to think about using skin care and to regularly test your skin for any suspicious moles or other injuries. Many men who work in outside workplaces, such as ranchers, construction workers, and truckers, are more deal with the sun, wind, and other elements that can directly produce painful conditions on the skin. Truckers may have one side of the face more harmed than the other, because of the sun from the window. Constructions workers may bear from extreme dryness, daftness, and even cracking and bleeding. Solving these skin problems can create going back to work the next day just a little bit easier.

(2) The TV advertisement may brings positive health body message after the skin health product users choose to buy its brand skin health product. So, the body attraction is very necessary to men in love and career. The tendencies are changing with the preparation habits of today's modern man. The motivation is that people are much more cognition of their appearances and want to be more attractive and appealing. Therefore, men have the trend to choose the skin care products to become.

So, when many TV audiences can watch TV image or pictures to let them to believe that they must give above skin health protection uf they use this brand of any kinds of skin health products. Then, this TV advertisement can persuade any age of skin health users to choose to buy its any kinds of skin health products more easily. Even, they won't feel to compare other brands of similar skin health products before they choose to buy which one is more suitable because TV advertisement is their first time contact channel to excite their skin health use choice need in perference. So, first time TV advertisement may influence any skin health users remember the brand of skin health product in long time memory. Then, when they go to any medicine shop to buy any kinds of skin health products, they must remember this brand of skin health product and enquire the salespeople whether this medicine shop can provide this brand of skin health products to let them to buy in preference. So, successful TV skin health product advertisement will bring long time memory to the brand of skin health product. Long time advertisement memory will be important factor to influence any skin health product users whose purchase choice preference in this competitive skin health product market.

Advertising is a way of communication to encourage an audience for making purchase decision about a product or service and conveying information to viewers. It is considered as a vital and essential element for the economic growth of the marketers and businesses (Ryans, 1996). Advertising is usually a paid form of exposure or promotion by some sponsor that reaches through various traditional media such as television, newspaper, commercial radio advertisement, magazine mail, outdoor advertising or modern media such as blogs, websites and text messages (Ahmed & Ashfaq, 2013).

Marketers have always adapted to changing business demands when it comes to creating new advertisements. The use of advertisements has significantly increased in the 20th Century as industrialization expanded the supply of manufactured products. However, not many businesses practiced advertising at the time. During the late 80s advertisements were fairly limited to television, radio, billboards and newspapers. In the modern times, businesses are leaning towards Digital Advertising. Companies are so focused in social media and mobile advertisements that they may take over Television advertisement very soon

Entertainment has been one of the primary criteria for creating an advertisement. Entertainment is used as a tool to gain attention of customers. An interesting and entertaining ad is more likely to be remembered by consumers rather than a boring one. Therefore, it can be said that entertainment increases the effectiveness of advertising. That is why many companies are investing a lot of money to make advertisements that are humorous (Mandan, Hossein & Furuzandeh, 2013). However, entertaining advertisements do not necessarily mean humorous ads. Thrilling, full of suspense advertisements can also be counted as entertaining. One of the biggest examples of all time is the Apple super bowl commercial "1984". It left people awestruck and it was immediately able to get attention of people. It was very effective in terms of spreading news about a new era of computers. It also had a huge part in generating sales for the company.

Familiarity to the brand of skin health product from advertisement channel

Alba & Hutchison (1987) defined familiarity as the number of product-related or service-related experiences that have been gathered by the consumer. These related experiences include direct and indirect experiences such as exposure to advertisements, interactions with salespersons, word of mouth contact, trial and consumption. Johnson and Russo (1984) viewed familiarity as being tantamount with knowledge. Johnson & Kellaris (1988) have considered experience contributing to familiarity. Review of the literature shows that knowledge; experience and familiarity are closely intertwined. Following Alba and Hutchison's (1987) definition, brand familiarity is identified as the accumulated correlated experiences that customers have had with a brand (Ballester, Navarro & Sicilia, 2012).

This means that advertisement does in fact affect the buying behaviour of consumers. Among the four independent variables however, we can see that Familiarity and Entertainment have the most significant impact. So, we can see that the psychological impact that Familiarity has on consumers does in fact lead to positive buying behaviour. In this case, most consumers have also taken Entertainment as a positive indicator towards a brand rather than negative.

'Advisement Spending' comes in third in terms of significance. This implies that people's association with 'Spending' and 'Brand' is likely to lead people to buy a product. In other words, advertisement spending is somewhat successful in persuading people to make a purchase. Social Imaging in Advertisement is seen to have the least impact. It means that people's desire to belong to a certain group sometimes makes people buy a product. But consumers are more concerned with other factors rather than the 'social imaging' in the advertisement.

Consumers are more motivated to buy a product when they see an advertisement of it somewhere; they also feel safe to buy a product that they have seen advertisement of. Consumer develops a level of trustworthiness for a brand they have seen advertisement of. They were even noted to collect information of products from advertisement, get to know about the usage and benefits of product and then make a purchase decision based on that. Therefore, advertisement is a very good marketing tool for generating more sales.

In conlcusion, thus, I believe that TV advertisment can be the most Familiar image or picture channel to the brand of skin health product because TV audiences can watch the performers' behaviors how they use the brand of skin health and they perform what skin health advantages that they feel from the TV picture images from television.

reference

Alba, J.W. & Hutchinson, J.W. (1987). Dimensions of consumer expertise. Journal of Consumer Research, 13, 411-454.

Ahmed, S. & Ashfaq, A. (2013). Imapct of advertising on consumer buying behavoiur through persuasiveness, band image and celebrity endorsement. Global Media Journal, 6(2).

Ballester, E.D., Navarro, A. & Sicilia, M. (2012). Revitalising brands through communication messages: The role of brand familiarity. European Journal of Marketing, 46(1/2), 31-51.

Johnson, R. & Kellaris, J. (1988). An exploratory study of price/

perceived quality relationships among consumer services. Advances in Consumer Research, 15, 316-322.

Johnson, E.J. & Russo, J.E. (1984). Product familiarity and learning new information. Journal of Consumer Research, 11, 542-550.

Mandan, M., Hossein, S. & Furuzandeh, A. (2013). Investigating the impact of advertising on customer's behavioural intentions. Business and Economic Research, 3(1).

Ryans, C. (1996). Consumer Resources. Journal of Small Business Management, 34, 63-65.